60 000 114 337

D0531536

Northamptonshire
DISCARDED
Libraries

tal

WAYLAND

**Northamptonshire Libraries
& Information Service**

60 000 114 337	
Peters	07-Mar-2011
C362.11	£5.99

First published
in 2011
by Wayland

Text copyright © Claire Llewellyn
Photograph copyright © Wayland
with the exception of cover background
© Istock, p6 © Istock, X-ray graphic
p14 © Istock and car graphic p18 © Istock

Wayland
338 Euston Road
London NW1 3BH

Wayland Australia
Level 17/207 Kent Street
Sydney, NSW 2000

The rights of Claire Llewellyn to be identified as the Author of
this Work have been asserted by them in accordance with the
Copyright, Designs and Patents Act, 1988.

All rights reserved

Series Editor: Louise John
Editor: Katie Powell
Design: D.R.ink
Photographer: Andy Crawford
Consultant: Shirley Bickler

A CIP catalogue record for this book is available from the British Library.

ISBN 9780750263757

Printed in China

Wayland is a division of Hachette Children's Books, an Hachette UK Company

www.hachette.co.uk

With thanks to the London Ambulance Service and Crowborough Memorial Hospital

Every effort has been made to clear copyright. Should there be any inadvertent omission,
please apply to the publisher for rectification.

Contents

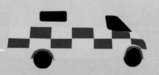

The fall

Last week I was riding my bike.
I went very fast.

Then I fell off with a big **bump**!
"Ow! My arm!" I screamed.

The ambulance

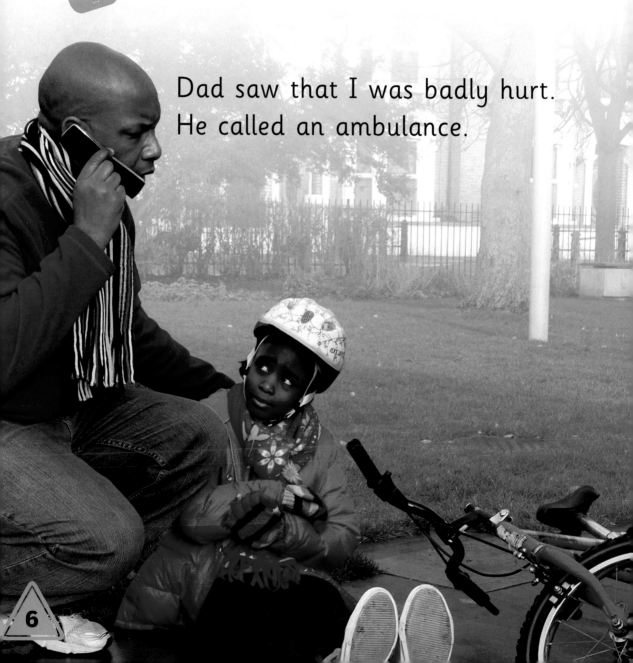

Dad saw that I was badly hurt.
He called an ambulance.

6

It came very quickly.
Its lights were flashing.

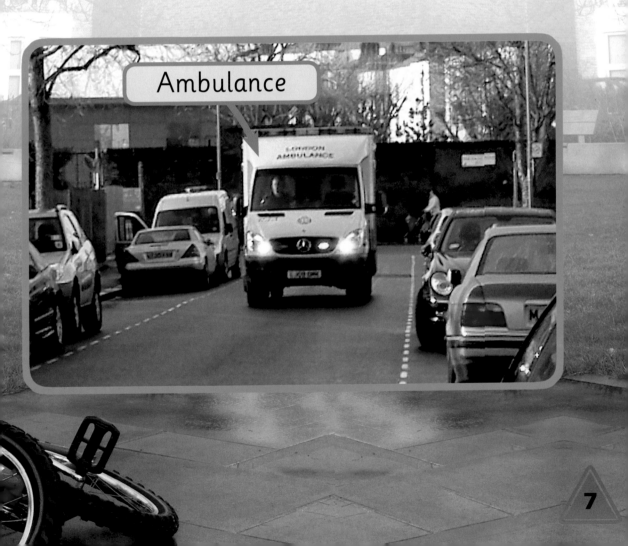

The paramedics

The paramedics looked at my arm.

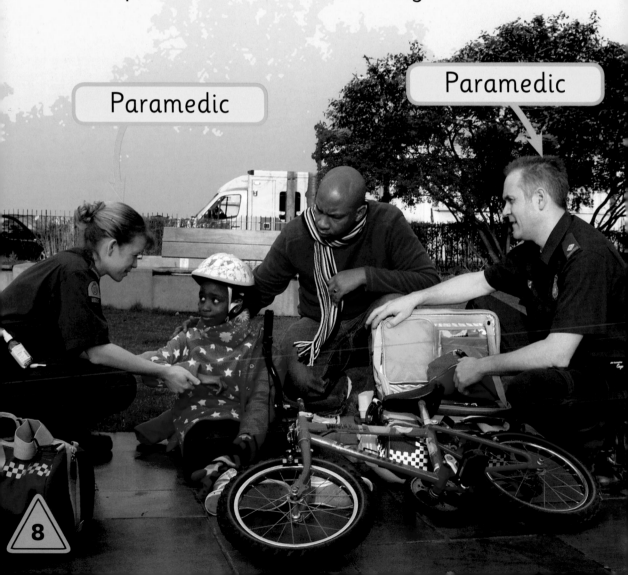

Paramedic

Paramedic

8

"You need to go to hospital to see if your arm is broken," they said.

In the ambulance

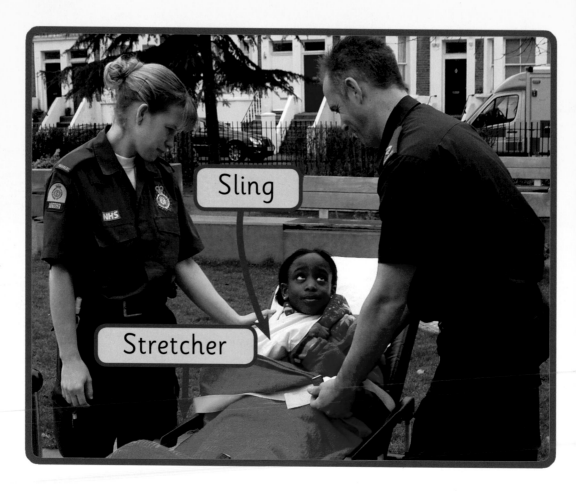

The paramedics put my arm in a sling and lifted me onto a stretcher.

Then they put me in the ambulance and they drove me to the hospital.

At the hospital

Dad and I went into the hospital.

Medicine

Nurse

A nurse came to see me.
She gave me some medicine
to stop my arm hurting.

13

The x-ray

Next I was sent for
an x-ray. An x-ray is
a photo of your bones.

A doctor looked at the x-ray.
"You have a broken bone," she said.

Doctor

X-ray

The cast

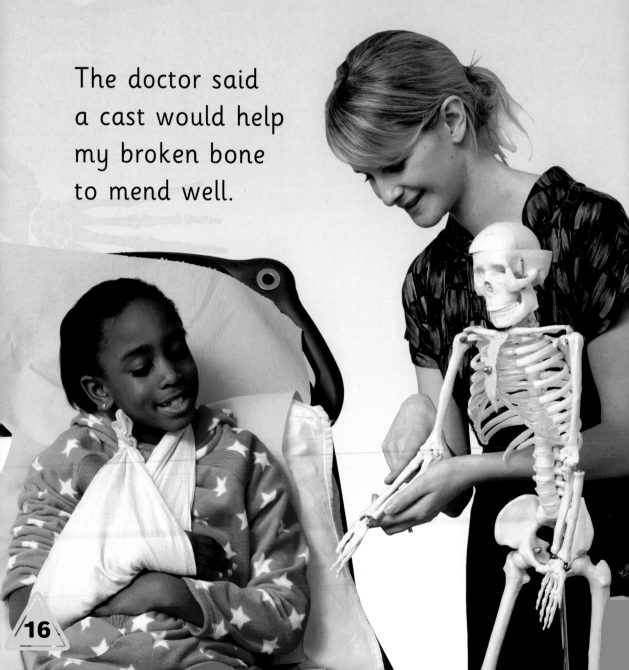

The doctor said a cast would help my broken bone to mend well.

A nurse put my cast on.

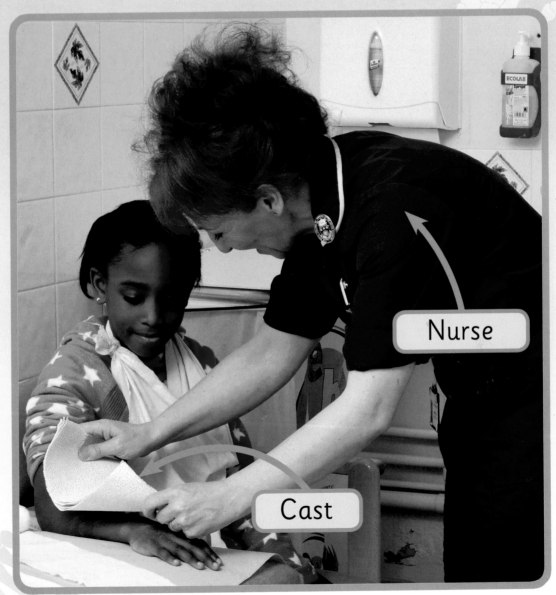

Nurse

Cast

Then it was time to go home.

The nurse said, "Come back in six weeks. Your arm will be better then, and I will take off the cast."

Being Careful

My arm still hurts
so I wear it in a sling.
Now I have to take care.

In five weeks' time my cast comes off,
and I'll be back on that bike!

Tell the story

These photos will help you tell the story of my broken arm. Can you put them in the right order?

START READING is a series of highly enjoyable books for beginner readers. **The books have been carefully graded to match the Book Bands widely used in schools.** This enables readers to be sure they choose books that match their own reading ability.

**Look out for the Band colour on the book
in our Start Reading logo.**

The Bands are:

Pink Band 1A & 1B

Red Band 2

Yellow Band 3

Blue Band 4

Green Band 5

Orange Band 6

Turquoise Band 7

Purple Band 8

Gold Band 9

START READING books can be read independently or shared with an adult. They promote the enjoyment of reading through satisfying stories and non-fiction narratives, which are supported by fun illustrations and photographs.

Claire Llewellyn has written many books for children. Some of them are about real things like animals and the Moon, others are storybooks. Claire has two children, but they are getting too big for her books now. She hopes you will enjoy reading them instead!